Looking at . . .
Chasmosaurus
A Dinosaur from the CRETACEOUS Period

THE NEW
DINOSAUR
COLLECTION

For a free color catalog describing Gareth Stevens' list of high-quality books,
call 1-800-542-2595 (USA) or 1-800-461-9120 (Canada).
Gareth Stevens' Fax: (414) 225-0377.

Library of Congress Cataloging-in-Publication Data available upon request from publisher.
Fax: (414) 225-0377 for the attention of the Publishing Records Department.

ISBN 0-8368-1345-6

This North American edition first published in 1995 by
Gareth Stevens Publishing
1555 North RiverCenter Drive, Suite 201
Milwaukee, Wisconsin 53212 USA

This U.S. edition © 1995 by Gareth Stevens, Inc. Created with original © 1995 by Quartz
Editorial Services, Premier House, 112 Station Road, Edgware HA8 7AQ U.K.

Consultant: Dr. David Norman, Director of the Sedgwick Museum of Geology,
University of Cambridge, England.

Additional artwork by Clare Herronneau.

Printed in the United States of America

1 2 3 4 5 6 7 8 9 99 98 97 96 95

Looking at . . . Chasmosaurus

A Dinosaur from the CRETACEOUS Period

by Heather Amery

Illustrated by Tony Gibbons

THE NEW
DINOSAUR
COLLECTION

Gareth Stevens Publishing
MILWAUKEE

Contents

Introducing
Chasmosaurus

Chasmosaurus (<u>KAZ</u>-MOE-<u>SAW</u>-RUS) may have looked fierce but, like all herbivores, it only ate plants. Nevertheless, if attacked, it would probably stand and fight rather than try to run away.

This dinosaur lived about 70 million years ago in Late Cretaceous times. The most noticeable thing about **Chasmosaurus** was the huge, knobby frill that covered its neck and shoulders. But was this a useful shield to protect **Chasmosaurus** from attack by a hungry, meat-eating dinosaur? Or was it just for show?

Where did scientists first find the bones of **Chasmosaurus**? And how much do they know about its behavior?

Turn the pages that follow to find out more about this prehistoric creature with the ornamental neck frill.

Frilled

Chasmosaurus also had an unusual mouth that looked like a parrot's beak.

Chasmosaurus lived in a part of the world that is now Alberta, Canada. It was as long as a big car and taller than today's average adult male. It lumbered along on four thick legs.

Take a look at its head frill first. Along the edge was a row of small, sharp bones. Its head had three horns. The shortest was above its nose. The other two horns were larger and more pointed, and above its eyebrows.

beast

It would bite off tough leaves and plants with its beak and chew them up with rows of flat teeth at the back of its jaws.

Chasmosaurus's body was bulky and round, and it had a thick tail — useful for giving a hard whack to enemies that came too close.

Chasmosaurus probably lived in small herds. A herd would wander about in search of fresh food to eat, continually moving on to new grazing grounds — and constantly on the lookout for fearsome predators seeking a tasty meal of raw **Chasmosaurus** flesh.

Horn-skulled

Chasmosaurus had a very strong skeleton to support its heavy body. But it was not built for speed. So although it had a powerful set of muscles to move its stumpy front and back legs, it could only plod along slowly.

8

skeleton

Chasmosaurus needed huge amounts of food to keep healthy and satisfy its appetite. The size of its ribs shows that it must also have had a big stomach to process all the plants and leaves it ate as a herbivore. Like all herbivores, it probably spent most of each day eating.

In its thick neck and around its strong backbone, Chasmosaurus had powerful muscles to hold up the weight of its long head and magnificent neck frill. As you can see, the neck frill was not solid bone but had gaps in it. These made it much lighter than it otherwise would have been. These gaps were probably filled with muscle, and the whole frill was covered with thick skin.

Chasmosaurus probably used its horns as weapons, in much the same way that rhinoceroses do today. Turn the page to find out what a Chasmosaurus fight must have been like!

9

Let the battle begin!

During most of the year, herds of **Chasmosaurus** lived peacefully together, grazing across their territory and looking after their young. But when the mating season arrived, the large adult males went to war, fighting each other to see who would mate with the females.

Two males would challenge one another, roaring and pawing at the ground with their front feet. They may also have raised their huge neck frills in a display of size and strength.

If this was not enough to frighten the smaller, weaker male, the two **Chasmosaurus** would then charge, trying to stab at each other with their long horns. Turning, they may then have lashed their tails. One hard blow might have been enough to break the opponent's leg.

As the rest of the herd watched, the fight would fill the air with dust and the smell of crushed plants. But the battle seldom ended in death. The two males were only trying to prove which was the stronger. The victor would then mate with the females.

Scavengers

Herds of **Chasmosaurus** found plenty of fresh leaves and plants growing in the lush valleys. But there was danger, too. Sudden heavy rainstorms sometimes caused flash floods. Without any warning, a great wall of muddy water would rush down a valley, drowning everything in its path.

A herd of dinosaurs feeding in the valley had no chance of escape.

The entire herd would be swept away by the torrent, later to become a meal for scavenging dinosaurs. One type of scavenger might be **Albertosaurus** (AL-<u>BERT</u>-OH-<u>SAW</u>-RUS), a huge, meat-eating dinosaur with great jaws and sharp teeth for chewing at flesh. It would be easy for **Albertosaurus** to break up a carcass. Two might even have fought to feed on a dead **Chasmosaurus**.

After a few days, all that would be left of the herd of **Chasmosaurus** would be gnawed and scattered bones.

13

The changing Cretaceous world

About 135 million years ago, in Cretaceous times, certain remarkable changes began to occur on Earth. The great landmass that scientists call a "supercontinent" had now begun to break up.

The landscape also started to look more like it does today. There were willows, oaks, poplars, and pine trees, as well as magnolias and holly, heather, and climbing roses.

A number of new dinosaurs had begun to appear, too — among them, dinosaurs with horns and frills like **Chasmosaurus**, shown here rearing up to scare off an approaching enemy while a pterosaur flies overhead.

15

Rescue mission

Led by a large male, a family group of **Chasmosaurus** lumbered across a valley, eating the low-growing plants. While the adults ate with their heads down, the young ones played at mock battles, squealing and butting at one another.

Swinging around, it saw a massive **Allosaurus** (AL-OH-SAW-RUS) racing toward the herd. The dreaded carnivore was hungry, and

It was an ordinary Cretaceous day. But every day held possible dangers for herbivores, so they constantly had to be on guard. Suddenly, a large male raised its head, sensing the approach of a carnivore.

its great jaws were open wide.

Grunting with alarm, the **Chasmosaurus** hurried toward the rest of the herd. Now they all sensed trouble.

Quickly, the adults pushed the young ones into a group, whacking them gently with their tails. Forming a ring in front of the young, they now turned to face the awesome predator.

Allosaurus came to a halt and walked slowly around the circle of fierce, horned heads.

Then, all at once, snapping its enormous jaws, the **Allosaurus** lunged at the nearest **Chasmosaurus**. But the pointed horns jerked upward, just catching **Allosaurus**'s outstretched neck and tearing the tough skin. The wound was painful and **Allosaurus** started to bleed. It had met its match.

It gave the occasional threatening growl and glared at the horned herbivores, challenging them to make a move. The **Chasmosaurus** glared back, lowering their horns ready for attack.

The giant dinosaur leapt backward, its huge claws scrabbling to grip the soft ground. Roaring with rage, it turned and walked away. Still hungry, it went off in search of another, weaker victim. The herd of **Chasmosaurus**, meanwhile, returned to its feeding grounds, ever alert.

The great head mystery

When scientists first began to study **Chasmosaurus**, they were puzzled. The skulls they had dug up all looked very much the same. All had the usual blunt nose horn and the two longer eyebrow horns.

But there were some that had much shorter nose and eyebrow horns. So were these two different dinosaurs, or were they perhaps the same dinosaur but with different-looking heads?

Fossilized skulls of these two types were found in the same place, along the Red Deer River, in Alberta, Canada. The one with short horns was given the name **Chasmosaurus belli**. The one with long horns was called **Chasmosaurus kaiseni**.

But since the remains of both these dinosaurs had been found in the same rocks, scientists decided they might be the males and females of the same species.

Many of today's horned animals have distinct differences in the horns of the males and females. So maybe **Chasmosaurus kaiseni**, with the big horns, was actually a male, and **Chasmosaurus belli** was the female.

The males and females may also have had slightly different coloring, as shown in the two illustrations here.

Chasmosaurus data

Chasmosaurus has a name that means "ravine" or "cleft face." Its body was bulky, with a strong backbone and firm muscles to support the weight of its large head. It must also have had a big stomach to hold the huge amounts of plant food it ate.

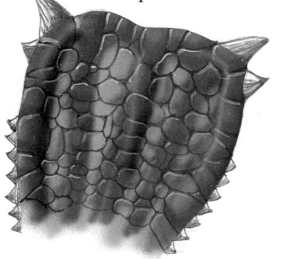

Magnificent neck frill

The huge neck frill covering **Chasmosaurus**'s back looked strong and had small, sharp bones along the edges.

But the frill was probably only useful for display. The larger a male's frill, the more it could impress other members of the herd.

Nose horn

Chasmosaurus had a small, blunt horn on its nose. The size of this horn varies on the skulls found so far. Those with smaller horns may have been females. Or perhaps they were young ones whose horns were still growing. Its big, broad head also featured a strong beak, useful for biting tough vegetation.

Chasmosaurus chewed its food with flat teeth at the back of its jaws. When a tooth wore down, it fell out, but this did not matter. Another grew in its place.

Stumpy legs

Chasmosaurus lumbered along on four thick, stumpy legs. Each foot had four short toes.

Powerful tail

Chasmosaurus had a tapering tail. It was thick and muscular, and helped balance the weight of this dinosaur's large head. The tail was strong enough to deliver hefty blows.

Brow horns

Over each eye, **Chasmosaurus** had a long, pointed horn, making it look quite fierce. Like the nose horn, these brow horns seem to have varied in size. The males probably found them useful weapons when warding off rivals or, perhaps, a predator.

Meet more Ceratopsids

Chasmosaurus (**1**) belonged to a group of dinosaurs known as **Ceratopsids** (SER-A-TOP-SIDS). **Triceratops** is a particularly well-known **Ceratopsid**. Most had sharp beaks, as well as horns and frills on their necks. Let's get to know some of the other **Ceratopsids**.

Protoceratops (PRO-TOE-SER-A-TOPS) (**2**) was much smaller than **Chasmosaurus**. It lived in Mongolia, where its nests have been found, complete with fossilized eggs. It had a fine head frill but no true horns.

Pentaceratops (PEN-TA-SER-A-TOPS) (**3**) was one of the largest members of the family. Its name means "five-horned face," but it had only three fairly large horns. The other two were small, hardly visible spikes on its cheeks.

Styracosaurus (STY-RAK-OH-SAW-RUS) (**4**) was about the same size as **Chasmosaurus**, but looked much fiercer.

Its name means "spiked reptile" because of the long spikes over its neck frill. It also had a long, upright horn on its nose and two small horns above its eyes.

Monoclonius (MON-OH-KLONE-EE-US) (**5**) was larger than **Protoceratops** and the first **Ceratopsid** to be found. Its name means "single shoot." It got this name from one tooth that was found in Montana about 150 years ago. Since then, several skeletons have been discovered. It had one large nose horn and, of course, a neck frill.

4

5

GLOSSARY

carcass — the dead body of an animal.

carnivores — meat-eating animals.

frill — a fringe or ruffle around the neck of an animal.

graze — to feed on grass or other plants that grow in a field or pasture.

herbivores — plant-eating animals.

herd — a group of animals that travels together.

lumber (v) — to move slowly and heavily.

mate (v) — to join together (animals) to produce young.

predators — animals that kill other animals for food.

remains — a skeleton, bones, or dead body.

scavengers — animals that eat the leftovers or carcasses of other animals.

skeleton — the bony framework of a body.

INDEX